Half-Life

Half-Life
Michael Hulse

2013

Published by Arc Publications
Nanholme Mill, Shaw Wood Road
Todmorden OL14 6DA, UK
www.arcpublications.co.uk

Design by Tony Ward
Printed in Great Britain by the
Berforts Information Press Ltd.

978 1908376 19 0 (pbk)
978 1908376 20 6 (hbk)

Cover photo: 'Gethsemane' © Tony Ward, 2011

ACKNOWLEDGEMENTS:

Poems in this book have been published in the *Irish
Times, Istanbul Review, Kenyon Review, London Magazine,
London Review of Books, Poetry Review, Poetry Salzburg
Review, Sport, Yale Review* and *The King's Lynn Silver
Folio: Poems for Tony Ellis.*

Editor for the UK & Ireland:
John W. Clarke

This book is for Kathrin and Agnes

I've loved it all my life,
the smell of baking bread,
and now it fills the house
as my daughter, all of two,
eagerly helps her mother
and proudly tells her father,
    "Agnes bake it."

We break the pith and crust
and raise a glass of wine
and talk of what we have done
and what we hope to do
and all of us together
humbly tell the father,
    "Homo fecit."

Contents

I
Freeman / 11

II
The Return / 15
The Syrian Bride / 17
A Carcass / 19
In Sant' Antonio di Padua / 20
Saskatoon / 22
Home / 23
Burj Khalifa / 24
Lagerfeld / 25
Wewelsfleth / 26
In the Peloponnese / 28
After the Warming / 29
From the Virtual Jerusalem / 30
Swiss National Day in Lavigny / 32
Rousseau in Staffordshire / 33
To Thine Own Self Be True / 35
Arse over Tip / 37
Quod Scripsi Scripsi / 39
A Virgin in Mexico City / 40
The Half-Life of Jesus / 42
The Swallows / 44
Eh, Tom? / 45

III
Foreknowledge Absolute / 49

IV
The Truth of Fiction (I) / 75
The Truth of Fiction (II) / 77

Author's Note / 79

Biographical Note / 81

I

Freeman

Freeman pulled over on the West Gate Bridge, in heavy traffic,
    says my friend,
with his kids in the back, the little girl, the boys,
and he walked round the car and pulled open the door
and he took out his four-year-old daughter
and lifted her and threw her off the bridge.

When he opened the door, did he hold out a hand, and speak
    to her reassuringly,
and smile as a father smiles when he knows there is nothing
    to be afraid of,
and take her, calmly, with death in his heart, and raise her,
    calmly, as any father
might, let's say, when his daughter dares the slide, alone, for
    the very first time,
when six feet are still the Empire State – calmly, teaching her trust?

You have to imagine it, says my friend –
the whole of it happens in full view
of six lanes of commuter traffic,
cars and trucks and vans are shrieking to a stop,
everyone sees him as he throws his daughter off the bridge.

I can imagine it. Nothing easier. Nothing more impossible.
But I remember how K and I were thrilled to see, on a hospital scan,
the beating heart of a life in the making, the life that became
    our daughter.
I remember the moment I saw her head appear.
I remember the cries her mother gave. The joyful agony.

It was the usual story, says my friend – revenge on a wife.
He drove to the family court and stood there witless with his boys,

Ben and Jack, hugging his trouser-legs, begging him to go
    back, Daddy, get her.
By then the police were wading into the mudflats by the riverbank,
and found the little girl. Alive. Who clung to living for an
    hour or two.

Please, I say, have mercy, please, oh no, please, not another word.
– But my friend will have none of it: Which of us knows what
    we are capable of?
There's evil in us all. It might so easily have been you,
    throwing the girl from the bridge.
Wasn't that you, climbing back in, snapping at the wailing
    boys, stepping on the gas?

They're wrong (I say), the witnesses – oh no, that wasn't me –
that was me down there, down there in the water, down there,
    far below,
standing in the shallows, waiting among the reeds and the
    waterfowl,

waiting with my arms outstretched to catch my daughter
    when she fell –
my shoes and trousers, look, are soaked, and caked with
    reeking mud –

there I was, at the dark river's margin, waiting as any father would.

II

The Return

A Carthage it wasn't; but this was a city of libraries and bars,
offices, hospitals, galleries, schools and arenas.
That cypress grows where the 34 bus used to stop.
That's what remains of the chamber of commerce. And that
was the headquarters of a software corporation.

I knew the place. But that was long ago,
and now the stories being written here
know nothing of urban planning or insider trading,
nor of collateral, nor of collateral damage,
nor of the pools where the damsel-fly sits once again on the
    lotus on long summer days.

They say that the souls of the dead inhabit the place.
They say there are shifts in the light, prints in the dust,
unravelling veils of vapour on the breeze,
whispers that tell of rememberings of the heart,
murmurs at night like the plainsong of the stars.

They say from the visible darkness, the nowhere of days,
a figure comes walking, into the limitless light,
gazing ahead into space as if all of his life
were dependent on what lay before him. As if
he saw now, as a thing he might touch, the past become present.

He has been to the place. The profundis. The night
where neither man nor woman has a name.
He has been to the place. To return her to life.
And now he walks as if the very air
threatened to snatch her back and keep her there.

Behind him, slender, wary, comes the other,
a faceless shape, muffled in heavy robes,
the hidden head in a cowl, the tread of the feet
soft as a footpad fox's by a henhouse. She
(if this is a she) has known the thing we know we cannot know –

not the confinement of miners at Copiapó,
not the democracy of survival, the ad hoc after-polity
complete with leadership, medic, official biographer,
communications manager, poet and pastor,
and lifelines to a world of bright return,

but darkness meaning darkness only darkness,
and solitary only solitary,
the sentence to be served in full,
the ever-after locked, the key thrown away,
"I am not that I am not" daubed in shit above the entrance.

He turns (for now they are clear of the dark, and he may),
turns to his bride, and reaches to throw back the cowl,
and I want to cry out, I want to say no. For I have seen
the lotus unfolding in summer sun, the shimmer of light in the rose,
the making of love, the building of homes, the children in the
        meadows.

But the cowl falls back. And Oppenheimer returns
to the site he has code-named Trinity, the place where he must become
the destroyer of worlds. The cowl falls back, the histories rewind,
across the synapses the last of living travels,
Zyklon-B goes back into production. And she (if

this is a she), she stretches her arms to claim him as her own.

The Syrian Bride

Night was breathing a cold kiss of dark on the nape of the day.
      A burnt-out APC. A crumpled flatbed. Men in scarves and combats.
Boys in doorways. Wreckage. I'd arrived.
      I stood for a while by the roadside,
watching a crow that plucked and stabbed at a carcass in the dirt.

Felt like I'd known the place for years. The stories about the place.
      The wreckage. The rubble. The helicopters chopping overhead.
The savour of death on my tongue. The town reeked
      of blood, destruction, a terrible love.
Like the slaughterer's slab at a sacrifice. I'd arrived.

House-fronts smashed, cables hanging, trucks crushed, rubble, blood,
      pockmarked walls, toppled masts. A finger in the road.
A plume of smoke like a prayer on the pitiless air.
      Whatever the people were praying for there,
the heavens didn't care.

I found the address. Neighbours said: She died this afternoon.
      The family, all of them, all are dead. You come too late. Now sleep.
They gave me bread. I ate. Then went
      alone to bed. And lay there. Aching. Listening. To
the smash and the squall of the silence of the night.

She came to me. My bride. The daughter of the ruined house.
      Her face was blasted. As if you had smudged
a drawing in ochre chalk. An arm was torn.
      Her breast was a flap of stuff. "You came
to marry hope," she said. "I'll tell you how I died.

"It happened after prayers. The tanks were firing on the neighbourhood.
          The army banged at everybody's doors.
My father answered ours. He was a soldier too, I told them.
          I showed them his ID. They shot him. My father's
brains spilled out like the brains of a dog in the road.

"My mother, my sisters, my brothers, the babies, all of us, all are dead.
          I started to crawl, and heard the cry
of my cousin, the darling little one, and snatched her to me,
          and ran out into the road, hugging her close.
And that is all I know.

"You came to marry a future. I am your future. I am your hope.
          Keep me alive," she said. "Don't let me die.
Don't let me die." – Her flesh was cold.
          We fevered. Fire and ice. Together.
Till the morning broke. And she was gone.

I went to see the bodies in their blankets. What remained to say?
          I left the place, and shook off the dust
from the soles of my feet, and stood for a while
          by the roadside, watching an ancient soul,
a familiar blackness, flapping, plucking, stabbing.

I knew that I must see my bride again.

A Carcass

Remember it, my soul –

that poem about a rotting carcass, an animal carcass, legs in the air
like the legs of the whores in the streets of Montmartre
when they've vanished up two flights of rickety stairs
and lie back on a mattress, the lamp turned down low –

an animal carcass, baking, roasting,
blackening in the heat of the sun,
blowflies flitting on flesh like the shifting of light on flowing water,
maggots seething and milling like souls

on the trams and trolley-buses of Paris
or Paradise (I had not thought death
had provided so well for so many) – an animal carcass,
the seething and rising and falling sending

a wave like a tide, like the rhythm of something alive,
like the music of life, through all of that putrefaction. Do
you remember? Cézanne had the poem by heart,
could recite it word perfect. Till he died. He knew

that the world that was reeling and seething and shifting
was humming with music like wind in a wheatfield.
Such you will be, he would say to the canvas,
after the last of the sacraments – paint an inch thick, etcetera.

In Sant' Antonio di Padua

Christ winked at me as I was on my way
to Sant' Antonio di Padua,
surprising me with an affable, almost roguish camaraderie –
winked from a hologram postcard that showed him

closing his eyes as he gave up the ghost
then opening now this one, now the other,
or even both at once, depending where I stood,
as if to say he was only fooling and wasn't really dead.

That week a Pope had gone to the Happy Vatican in the sky.
The basilica was a stir of pilgrims and tour guides, a bustle of
    grieving and prayer.
Stewards were making a clatter, setting out wooden collapsible chairs
for the swollen congregation they expected at a vigil.

Among the school of supplicants that shoaled about the shrine
I watched a woman, thirty-something, business suit and pearls,
pressing a sheaf of paperwork against the reliquary –
she lip-served in silence as if she were giving a blow-job to a lizard.

The Catholic church! – I've always had a soft spot for its comedy,
its hotchpotch of the silly, the rotten, the true, the outlandish,
    the downright horrific.
All of the kitsch! The bones behind glass! The everlasting chapels
papered with testimonials to the Virgin's intercession.

The first time ever I told a lie was in the confessional.
The first woman ever I fell in love with, ever desired, was a nun.
The first man ever whose brutal ways I detested was a priest,
an Irishman with a hacksaw voice and a harsh, abrasive smile.

How I thrilled to the ritual hiss of "those that trespass against us",
sibilants pissing through Mass like the Trinity at the Eternal Urinal.
How I rejoiced at the thought of piecing the whole of the scattered
    man together
when I saw, in the Hofburg at Vienna, one of John the Baptist's teeth.

A Jesuit lent me *And Then There Were None*
which I finished in terror at four a.m. in a room in a German pension.
Another Jesuit, when I was fifteen, wanted me to go to his place.
Another, Canadian-Irish, taught me the Gaelic for pullet shit.

The church was a giver and taker, a helper and harmer, a friend and foe.
It taught... not love, which had purer sources, but love-despite-the-
    evidence.
I learned to love not only the man on the cross, the supplicant
    woman, the vendors of cards,
not only the canny cardinals elsewhere, affecting to be above ambition,

but the whole of the terrible comedy in Altichiero's *Crucifixion* here,
where a man who has simply done a job of work has turned to walk away,
making his way through the crowd, his thoughts on other things already,
the hammer with which he drove in the nails tucked carelessly into
    his belt.

Saskatoon

for Dionne Brand

I bought a ticket to another country,
packed my death, and headed for the airport.

At check-in my mother asked me if I'd packed my bags myself.
She looked as she did when she sat me on her lap.

Read me a story, I said,
but she cried like a two-year-old and lay on the floor.

My father hoped I would have a nice day
and returned to his Latin primer, moving his lips.

Blum blum blum. Bli blo blo.
Carthage was levelled with the dust as we lifted into the heavens.

A flight without rest. A maculate conception.
A place without verbs, like Saskatoon.

Home

One day we realised the house had died.
We walked from room to room lamenting.

The undertaker came to measure it.
Cardboard'll do fer cremation. No need fer brarse 'andles.

The whole of the street sent flowers.
We kept the cards and letters of condolence in a shoe-box.

We've learned to live with the loss. But, truth to tell,
it's harder than ever to take the home insurance agents,

the double glazing salesmen on the doorstep,
the councillor coming knocking in the week before an election,

bewildered friends who find us here in empty vacancy
and shake their heads as we reply, *Where else would we be but home?*

Burj Khalifa

Not a pretty sight, this Aeolian spindleshanks of a building.
A crayfish's idea of a steeple. Or an instrument God's dentist
    might have used.

Like all of our attempts to scratch at heaven,
it rests on a foundation in the sand.

Filthy rich is as filthy rich builds.
Capital giving God the finger.

Lagerfeld

                              – I met him at a party,
the fashion designer we see in photos of shows
stomping ahead of the models down the catwalk,
pig-tailed, bullet-headed, wearing shades,
Teutonic with a *cosa nostra* air.
At first I thought him as humourless as they come,
but presently I realised I was wrong
when he strolled to the next room, which was empty,
a foxy grin at the corners of his mouth
as the crowd of hangers-on promptly followed,
vacating one room, filling the second,
like water poured from one bucket into another.

It reminded me of an account I once read
of President Andrew Jackson's inauguration,
when all the new-breed Mid-West democrats
tramped about the White House in their boots,
belching and farting and smashing the Ming,
till a vat of punch was deposited on the lawn,
which drew them off (so a diplomat wrote,
wrinkling his nose) as flies are drawn
to (euphemistically) honey.

Wewelsfleth

It is the sort of North European village
where storks from Spain or Morocco might spend the summer
and writers might settle to savour the bracing quiet.
Did anyone ever grow wealthy in this place?
The fishermen's crofts along the dykes
are simple homes, and those who have lived in the farmsteads
that stand like stranded hay-wains
stuck at the ends of lanes of pollard willows
won't ever have made much more from the land
than the wittering sheep that crop the grass.

"It's the fourth largest in the world," says our friend,
as we walk to the deepwater fleet that flows into the Elbe,
the fleet from which the village takes its name.
He means the enormous yacht that is under construction in the dock.
It is three times the height of any building anywhere in sight.
I'd pictured something forty feet long, with sails,
but this is the size of a North Sea ferry plying out of Hamburg.
"The American who thought he wanted it
tired of it quickly and sold it on to a sheikh.
The sheikh had marble flooring laid throughout.
It added tons to the displacement. When *he* got rid of it,
the present owner, another billionaire,
had all the marble ripped right out again.
Might as well burn your millions. Still, it means jobs."
An army of hard-hatted fitters and welders,
engineers with clipboards, men in overalls or suits,
are swarming under the cantilevered gantry of a crane.
"That camp of cabins has doubled the population.
Watch for the numberplates. Spanish. Polish. Everybody's here."

We walk on past the dock to where the fleet flows into the Elbe.
The muscled waters gather. Strong and confident and old,
the river writes no chronicles, affords no consolation:
it has only the beauty and might of a natural thing, no more, no less.
The tree-line on the farther bank, a half-hour ferry ride away,
is fading into April warmth and haze
where light and land and water meet and marry.

Nothing I see I own. And nothing would I wish to own.

In the Peloponnese

At the next table, grizzle-jowled, silver-haired, in his undershirt,
before a proprietorial spread
of zuccini, tomatoes, peppers, an Amstel beer, and a napkin of bread,
taking his elbowed ease for a lonely and difficult day at sea ahead
now that the weekend Athenians have departed,
the owner of the Panorama restaurant's at meat.

Aleppo pines and cypresses and figs
gentle and tremble and make a shade
where a cat the colour of Pericles
on the old one-hundred drachma note
rhetorically purrs *what price the Euro?*
to an imaginary parliament of fowls.

The nets are drying on the wall,
the water talks of love, I think, but not of currency,
and nothing, believe me, nothing at all
depends or ever could depend, on earth, in heaven or in hell,
on the cherry-tomato Fiat Seicento
parked on the seafront before the Apollo Hotel.

After the Warming

A Peruvian muleteer and his mule, in the panniers
the infamous missing X-rated reels of *The Sound of Music*;
a princess of one of the nameless lost cities of Mali,
wearing her hair in a Zelda Fitzgerald bob;
Parmigianino's copy of Ashbery's *Self-Portrait in a Convex Mirror*
with all of the artist's autograph annotations;
Percy Shelley, the one and only, whom we thought drowned,
with the *Poems* of Jorie Graham thrust back hurriedly into his pocket;
the famous lost Aztec washing-machine
with its drum in the form of an almost-perfect wheel
capable even then of 1200 revolutions per minute;
Nero's fiddle, Potemkin's village, Occam's razor, Buridan's ass,
and my grandmother's false teeth, made, like most modern dentures,
not of hippopotamus or walrus ivory
but of polymerized acrylic resin –

no, I can't pretend that anyone was prepared
for the things that came to light as the glaciers melted and the ice receded,
the things that fetched up scattered in streets and gardens
like beer-cans and burger-boxes on a Sunday morning.

From the Virtual Jerusalem

I

From darkness we come, to darkness return.
And in the interim we burn.

II

I never made the Bata Shoe Museum
to see the baby shoes of Leopold the Second.

III

Backs to *The Finding of the Saviour in the Temple*,
two men in middle years discuss their mortgages.

IV

These things have occupied me too:
the starry sky above, the moral law within.

V

Not the eternal city but an everlasting bore.
Not the New Jerusalem. The New Singapore.

VI

Suffer the bloody children to play their dumb computer games.
Why should I care if they remember how to spell their names?

VII

The night is an oil-slick
and I am a sea-bird.

VIII

Feels like I've been here forever, listening to Haile Selassie's valet
remember nothing worth remembering.

IX

The heart is snow. Year after year
we shovel the bloody driveway clear.

X

Uh-oh, here comes Big Baby,
crushing the bank on the corner under his great clodhopping feet.

XI

The time of my life
is having me.

Swiss National Day in Lavigny
for Sophie and Tatiana Kandaouroff and Jens-Martin Eriksen

Cities burn, favelas rot, the starving walk for water,
    elections are rigged and revolutions hijacked,
        tanks are deployed against the people – but
            here the children walk with lanterns

along the lane between the grocery and the château,
    they babble past the church, they know the life to come
        is this moment, this one, this one, and this,
            here – catch! They *are* the life to come

as they prattle and scatter across the darkening field.
    The language of the speeches says "audacity"
        and "tolerance" and "solidarity"
            but while the parents clap and blab

the children are inheriting as the birds inherit.
    They are not bankers, vintners, civil servants; they
        do not spin or toil; they skelter and skirl
            in polities not of the world

that their parents inhabit with their grown-up words and ways.
    How hard we have striven, all of us, all these years,
        millennia, to make the happy place:
            for *that* is the end of all we

think and all we do – a village much like this, where a bonfire
    burns, but neither books nor men. Is this the good life
        that makes heaven pointless? This still remains:
            to become as little children

skittering fast and light in the peace of the night.

Rousseau in Staffordshire

I think him one of the worst of men – a rascal (Johnson said).
      I would sooner sign a sentence for *his* transportation
than that of any felon. Yes,
      I should like to have him work in the plantations.
And Johnson hadn't seen Rousseau wearing Armenian dress.

Rousseau moved in to Wootton Hall, an isolated house.
      Pasture. Rabbit warrens. Sheep.
The most beautiful land in the world, said Rousseau.
      The local people had a rhyme, it seemed:
Wootton under Wever, where God comes never.

Thérèse for company. His "gouvernante" (so Hume declared).
      One day (Rousseau was living in the past)
I hid near the well where the girls of a house
      drew water. I offered the girls a sight
that was laughable rather than seductive.

He played the harpsichord. Walked his dog, Sultan. Sat under the oaks.
      Longed for Mme de Warens.
That sweetest intimacy. "Little one" was my name,
      hers "Mamma". One day I made her spit out a morsel –
I seized it and gobbled it up.

Thérèse quarrelled with the kitchen women. Rousseau sat under his oaks.
      Sempstresses, chambermaids, shop girls
hardly tempted me. Every man has his taste,
      and I have mine. On this point Horace and I
are of different persuasions.

Rousseau met Lady Andover, Lady Cowper, the Duchess of Portland,
      and Mary Dewes and her flock of lambs.

He thought of nightingales, grasses, flowers – a loveliness unknown
        in the melancholy land where he lived now.
His letters, he insisted, were opened, his food adulterated, money pilfered.

Once near Lausanne (he remembered), penniless, famished,
        he dined and slept at an inn
and breakfasted next morning. Couldn't pay.
        The good-natured innkeeper shrugged it off.
How worthy was that honest man's humanity!

He is a curiosity, an English lady wrote: his works
        extremely ingenious, as I am told, but
under the guise and pomp of virtue
        his sentiments are unorthodox and wrong.
The devil, concluded Rousseau, is welcome

to Wootton under Wever.

To Thine Own Self Be True

The delicate woman beside me on the flight
is reading *How to Win Friends
and Influence People*,
a book I believe I have known of all my life
but have never seen anyone read.
She is half the body mass of the man in the seat on her other side.
Her nose and mouth and chin are thin.
They taper like a pangolin's.
Her hair has been carefully taken up and pinned –
it bears all the signs of meticulous attention.
She is wearing a charcoal business suit –
a pencil skirt
of the sort I feel sure would attract the word "classic" –
and creamy, probably "classic" shoes,
and pearl studs in her ears,
which may be "real" or may be merely "cultured".
Her fingers are whitened with what looks like fear,
Platonic fear. She is a bobbin
wound-around with panicky inwardness,
bound in hard and tight into a fastness of herself.
Or, she is like an armadillo.
Down to the fingernails.
Her forefinger follows the text. Her lips
are shut so the blood has fled, as if to prevent them from moving.
She's reading as a Lutheran might read the word of God.
She's hard at work on an inner self
which, for all I know to the contrary,
may well have attractions like those of her physical self –
it may be petite as well,
it may wear the vestments of power
over a slender attenuation,
a tremor of the senses.

I could suppose that the physical self she's created
is a perfect match for her imagined self,
articulates exactly what she thinks she "really" is,
and it could also be the case
that what the book is telling her to seem
may coincide, with neither strain nor angst, with what she wants to be –
and one day, when she's learned whatever lessons it can teach her,
she will embody the paradox
of insincerely appearing to be the thing she sincerely is.

Arse over Tip

European Translators' College, Straelen

This language-fetishist retreat
in small-town Germany
has books as an ostrich has lice, a hundred and twenty
    thousand of them.
The books infest the atrium. The seminar rooms. The passages.
The study bedrooms are full of them. In mine, Hungarian
    literature. And French
from R to Z. Their languages
tremble with desire, as Barthes, I've no doubt, would have
    said. Now there
was someone who knew what he wanted. Or wanted to say.
    But what I really
want is you. Now. Against the shelves, say, so Babits Mihály and
Ady Endre (their names are arse over
tip) come
tumbling. Sprawl on the floor. Milan's a mild-mannered man. He's
re-translating *Joseph and his Brothers* into Croatian. Back in the
    dissident days
he did his time in gaol. With him
I have pleasant talks about comedy. Mischa's a mushroom-gatherer.
They know about mushrooms in Russia. He tells me
how to distinguish something from something else. And so another
ten or fifteen precious minutes of life
pass harmlessly enough. But
what I really want
is to love you so the teeth knock in your head. The
secretaries chainsmoke in the open spaces. Irmgard
asks if emplotment means anything more
than plot or plotting. I check the passage, say no, it's the usual
academic self-importance. Come to me, love. Come
sit on my laptop

and give back the meaning
to enter, hard return, control and shift. Come. Translate me.
Come make the word flesh. Come
come.

Quod Scripsi Scripsi
European Translators' College, Straelen

All these dictionaries! – in passageways, the TV room, everywhere! –
anywhere you might suddenly need to know
the something-else for something. Serbian-Icelandic,
Spanish-Croat, English-Thai, Tibetan-German. So many beautiful
flurries and blizzards and sandstorms of words. So many
weatherly ways of getting lost
in the world. So many
wuthering seductions. Lingua's
a woman, of course. Of course she has a way
of wearing high heels for a trek through the veldt.
She says, "Did you bring a map?"
It's hot. She hitches her blouse up and knots it.
Now her ice-cream starts to drip.
She sucks her thumb.
Don't get ideas. These are just words. This is language
writing the poem on auto-Pilate. Jesting. Playing
with itself. Washing its hands. And
idling. Ticking over. Doing nothing. Thinking nothing. Finding
mischief, as it always does, for idle words to do.

What I have written the language has written for me.

A Virgin in Mexico City
for Jennifer Clement and Victor Manuel Mendiola

As I walked out that morning from the Hotel La Casona
I was thinking, or I think that I remember I was thinking,
that the world is its own poem
and needs no writing into existence
by you, let's say, or me. I walked
a block or so along Durgano
thinking how little use the city had
for any reflections of mine on its wealth, reflections on its poverty,
so desperately, equally apparent,
how very little use the city had
for poems written by a visitor,
and one so briefly there.
                                        I found
myself, let's say, at a rotonda.
From it, six avenues radiated. For a while
I stood by a gas station in the triangle formed by two of the roads.
Notices by the pumps read *Apague el motor*.
Men in green overalls were filling up.
At the tapering point of the wedge, close to the traffic,
a shrine the size of an infant's coffin, painted white,
with two tall cypresses before it, and red roses,
was enclosed in a low box hedge.
High above was a sign reading PEMEX,
advertising Premium and Magna grades of gas.
Inside the shrine, in a padlocked glass case,
an unprepossessing plaster Virgin stood behind a vase of lilies,
in glory.
          If
you say the scene was unremarkable
I shall be tempted to agree, and I shall disagree,
for I was thinking then, and I think now,

of humble domestic altars with candles, joss and blossoms
lodged on the walls of Bangkok blocks
between the air-con and the fire escape,
and I was thinking of wayside shrines in Europe,
a statue of the Virgin carried home from Lourdes
on the back of a pilgrim who built a chapel for her,
a panorama of Jerusalem
painted for the fourteenth station of a Calvary,
and I thought then, and I think now, although I can't say what
    the thinking means,
that the universal spirit lives in glory, and is great, and will be known.

The Half-Life of Jesus

I

On the day when a survey of biblical knowledge
revealed that twenty per cent of respondents
who claimed to be Christians and to own a Bible
could say nothing whatsoever about
the crucifixion or the resurrection,
a brother of Michael Jackson said his name would live forever.

II

From the Ethiopians on the roof,
closest to God, I descended
to the patchwork of persuasions in the church
and stood in line for thirty minutes
waiting my turn to enter the horrible box
atop the sepulchre
where prayers and kisses
lip-glossed and glorified the rock –
the Lord, I suppose, knows why I was there,
he sees into the hearts of atheists –
and when I was the next at last
a great Greek momma hung with gold and rosaries and crosses
shoved like a hippo to the front
and, challenged by a shy, polite attendant
who pointed to the hundred others waiting,
brushed aside all fear of falsehood
as she might a parking ticket
and lied, "Young man, I've been here all the time!"

Church of the Holy Sepulchre, Jerusalem

III

These olive trees, which those who know such things
declare to be two thousand summers old ...
what ragged twists of wood they are,
like hanks of tangled rope, snagged, knotted, frayed,
the military grey-green of the leaves
silvered like suede brushed hard against the light.

Today there are men on knuckled wooden ladders
gathering in the bitter harvest,
dappled by the shadows and the sunlight,
knocking down the olives with their sticks.

What would I give to hear what they could say,
these trees, the sole surviving witnesses.

Garden of Gethsemane

IV

No, I can't suppose the Great Story true.
Still, I prefer to live as if it were.

And so I make the toilsome journey too,
with gifts of gold and frankincense and words.

The Swallows

The swallows, yes. Theirs is a world without ifs.
The feathers of their backs return to God
the colour of the element he lives in,
a slaty blackness with a touch of blue,
a darkness that is intimate
with what we like to call the infinite,
that known, unknown and other place
we study when the glass reflects our face.

They are all purpose. When they fly,
they fly as if it were no more odd
that a creature should live with no means of support
than that a creature unsupported should die,
as if to leave like a prodigal and to loft
on the merest of air to the merest of air,
in the knowledge that living is everywhere,
were a birthright, not (as we have supposed) a sin.

And, on the breast, their downy undersoft
is that Carrara quarry hue
I've seen in fading roses or in clover,
the colour of those chalky cliffs
not far along the coast from Calais' port,
the other side of where the land
was parted from the land, and waters wrote their name in sand,
and souls from nowhere followed, over Dover.

Eh, Tom?

Goethe in Venice knew what he wanted to hear:
the words of Ariosto, and of Petrarch,
sung on the waters by the gondoliers
to melodies of their own making – words
borne up on the lips of the living, as certain
as birds that the effortless air would bear them up.

The custom was already dying. Thirty years later,
Byron was saddened to find the tradition lost:
the gondoliers no longer sang their classics. I suppose
on another occasion his thought may have been of Venice,
with Moore, when a boating party passed them
singing the Irishman's words: "That's fame, eh, Tom?"

The singing has died. But the love is never lost,
the spiriting hope to make a thing that endures,
a thing that will stand, to be walked around and *seen* –
the longing to return to virgin fire,
to the elements that give all we make its birth,
the soil of a natural growth, the nurturing earth,

to gather all the sunlight on the water
into a marriage of artifice and nature,
an Amber Room that might survive itself
as the idea of a tower would outlive Pisa –
to *be* the air Sheherezade was breathing,
the light by which Leonardo painted Lisa.

III

Foreknowledge Absolute

I

What a swell party this is.
– I'm sorry, I don't think we've met?

Her smile is the melt of a snowflake in hell.
Her eyes are the burn everlasting.

The starlight at her ears and throat
had ceased to be before I noticed it.

She's wearing the new black. Her heels are like ice-picks.
Her skirt is of charcoal and ash. Her talk

is of body parts hung in the trees,
arms in the branches, a torso, a head impaled –

I was there, I saw it. She speaks of a truth
within all of the higgledy-piggledy relative anything-goes of truths,

the need to know your way through to the absolute.
Next July we collide with Mars. Call me Death, she says.

II

Sometimes I think I remember the start of it all,
she says (we are telling each other about our lives) –

that sense of having followed someone or something
truly preposterous, inconceivable, into an unknown place,

that sense of having fallen
a very long way down, a very long way down indeed,

down what you might call a wormhole (there's more
in heaven and earth than is dreamt of in your metrics).

On the way down I snatched from a passing shelf
a volume of *Classical and Quantum Gravity*

and read up quickly on what I thought or imagined was happening to me
and only stopped when a footnote cited the *Summa Theologica*

at which point, overcoming the fear
of killing someone, I dropped the book.

Whenever I think I remember the start of it all
what comes to mind is that seemingly endless fall,

the archives of the obsolete, the libraries of vanished thought,
the empty begging-bowls of past and present and to come –

I shall think nothing of tumbling down stairs,
I said to myself (says Death). Have you been listening to a word I've said?

– The *Quantum Theologica*?
– Don't be facetious. – Do that again, I like it.

III

One uneventful late October dusk
when failing sun was golden in the leaves

my father (she says), in his great-coat and boots,
umbrella in the one hand and portmanteau in the other,

put his foxy whiskers round the door
and casually told my mother

he'd to go up-country, and might not be back tomorrow.
And fired off a Parthian kiss. And was gone.

I heard the street door shut, and stretched, and twisted in the womb.
My mother sat and welcomed in the darkness to the room

and months went by and she was brought to bed.
They held me up. I screamed. And she was dead.

And he was elsewhere, always – all
of my childhood, all of my youth, for all

of the three-leggèd races, piano lessons,
the speech days and parties and school trips to Paris,

the rise and fall of empires, plagues in Egypt, moving pictures,
trials by the Inquisition, extraordinary rendition –

till one day, when the house itself
had long since wearied of the waiting

and didn't expect an end to the emptiness,
even loved its widowhood because it liked to wear the weeds,

the man who stepped aside from life and lost his place for ever
slipped his key into the lock, and opened the door, and called
    "I'm home!"

These last few days, says Death, have taken her back
to her childhood, all of those dreadful Ash Wednesdays,

streets deserted, streamers loose, confetti blowing about, now and then
an old woman in a head-scarf making her labouring way to church.

I'd never been to a children's ball.
I'd never worn costume. Never a mask.

I'd never worn lipstick or rouge (she tells me).
Yes, I was still a child.

That year, a friend was having a dress made,
made for the carnival, made by her mother

from pink crepe-paper, endless sheets of it, made to look like
    petals of roses,
the innermost tenderness of the innermost secret of the rose.

And then my friend's mother offered to make me
a rose-petal dress as well, says Death.

I'd have what I wanted. For three days, for carnival,
I would be somebody else.

We talked and we talked it until we were sore with the thought.
We would wear underslips, we decided, so

if it should rain
and our crepe-paper dresses

disintegrated
at least we'd be decent.

We talked it, we talked
and were sore with the thought

of a downpour, torrential, a terrible drenching,
the two of us girls in the street wearing nothing but flimsy
    wet underthings.

v

This is a story I'm sure you have heard,
says Death (as she brushes her lips on my cheek,

her fingers busy with my belt) – a story
about a girl, the usual girl,

taking the usual path through the forest
and meeting the usual stranger,

a wolf full of questions and hunger,
a grin like a Chevy, all teeth.

Some say the wolf runs ahead of the girl
and hides in the bed with a headful of horrors.

Some say the girl makes her visit, returns,
and surprises her mother

entwined on the sofa
with somebody muscular and furred.

Some say the girl makes her visit, returns –
her mirror shows her yellow-eyed and wiry,

the hair breaking out on the backs of her hands and her neck,
the drooling hunger dripping from her muzzle.

Still others doubt there ever was a wolf.
They say she was always all talk and her skirts were short.

Me (she says), I know that girl, I know her well –
now you lie there and don't you say a word.

A Frenchman talked to me at length of eating human flesh
which, he declared, had a flavour like pork preserved in nutmeg oil.

Negroes, he told me (says Death), were charming and gentle.
Like young rabbits. Those were his words. We gave them whisky,

and when they were drunk we slaughtered them.
He was bound for Tonkin. To shoot peacocks, he said.

A man from Prague (she laughs as she remembers)
told me his son had woken one morning to find himself transformed.

Into a roach. He wore uniform, this man – blue, with gilt buttons,
the kind of impossible collar they call a Vatermörder,

and on his cap was a monogram in gold. One day, he said,
when all the unpleasantness was over, we took the tram

to the outskirts of the city, my wife and my daughter and I,
and agreed to put all our troubles behind us, and look to the
    future again.

An archivist (retired) of Sárszeg dreamt of his daughter dead –
head shaven, mutilated, stab wounds to the breast –

then strolled down the main street to lunch at the King of Hungary,
rejoicing in the pepper pot, the mustard jar, the laundered tablecloth,

the basket of crusty rolls, salted croissants, small white
    poppy-seed loaves,
the apples and peaches, and the vanilla slices.

This is a story I read in a book (she says) –
you can't begin to imagine how many stories like this I've heard.

A Red Army officer opens a German closet
and fumbles his way through the clothes to the back

and encounters a woman, her warmth, her hair –
he has the impression she's naked under her dress.

The writer of the book's a woman. Say we call her J.
A German woman. Her people know all of the stories.

She's thought about power. She's thought about women,
        thought about men.
So this is what J, the writer, writes: that the woman,

the woman in the closet, I mean (says Death),
pushes the officer's head between her legs

and the Russian, a youngster, perhaps with a girl of his own
        back in Moscow,
he thrusts in his tongue. And she pisses all over his face.

Shall we pause at this point to think over the options?
We know what this man may have done. And what he may do.

We know of the blood he may have on his hands. And we know
there are uses for pistols, for rifles, for bayonets. So:

he's kneeling there letting it happen. She pisses
all over his face and he's kneeling there letting it happen,

callow young fellow who knows too much, who knows too little,
who knows what he's done, who knows what his men have done,

who knows what the woman's countrymen have done,
and his tears start to flow, and she speaks to him gently,

in softly-softly comforting motherly tones. And that (says Death)
has the feel of the end of the story. Or the beginning of the end.

This, give or take, more or less, is how J, the writer, tells it in
     her book.
Or isn't. So what happens next? Does the woman

(a) reach into the officer's holster
while he's distracted, and blow out his brains,

or (b) knock the lad down, haul out his member, and
briskly impale herself on it, or (c) point him to where

her husband is cowering under the boiler,
and make a suggestion the officer can't refuse?

One of these outcomes leads J to write:
finally death has been brought to its knees.

Yeah right. So now you see (she says)
what poor deluded boobies story-tellers are.

VIII

You know those little moments (she says)
that feel as if they could get out of hand and suddenly be
      something big?

There was this time in Turkey when my camera was stolen.
I know what you're going to say – that it's wrong

to want the passing moment to stand still.
I have a thing about arrested motion.

The camera was on the seat beside me with my bag
and when we reached Priene it was gone.

We stopped a couple of times, someone
could easily have lifted it out the window when I was looking away.

Police? Sure I told the police. I was there for two hours.
They took the details down three times.

They were kind of friendly, but my passport vanished.
A man brought me tea and asked if he could take a look at my shoes.

He held them in his hands, and his eyes were round, and he
      stroked them in awe,
as if they were a relic of the Prophet.

Ferragamo shoes, in case you want to know. He wanted me to
      mail him a pair
for his wife, but he couldn't afford the price.

He rubbed my left earlobe between
his forefinger and thumb

as if he was feeling cloth
and I began to get frightened.

You don't have to think I scare easily. Still,
I felt it was time I had my passport back.

I'm a beautiful woman, I'm not stupid, I'm young, I'm fun to be with,
and – ask me no questions – I'm rich as well.

Look at this hat. Italian. Look at the styling.
Nobody buys a Turkish straw hat.

IX

It was Friday, twelve twenty, New York (she remembers).
Nineteen fifty-nine. I watched him

one foot raised for a black who was shining
his shoes on the sunny side of the street,

I watched him in the bookstore and the bank,
the man-about-town from Maryland

with his Clark Kent jaw and his Woody Harrelson nose –
now that was the kind of man I could go for (she says)

with his junk lunch, his smoking, his smart taste in reading,
his ostentatiously no-frills writing.

I liked that light-heeled singer too, I
liked her so much she stopped breathing and

I watched as he paused for the newspaper picture –
I said: he'll be mine, he'll be mine.

x

Things are always happening (she says as we lie in the dark).
There was the year I was living in Lima.

The man I was with had stormed out in a temper.
I sat there drinking his whisky. Then the doorbell rang.

I know you don't just open the door in Lima.
We were living by a square where dope changed hands,

one side of us was the regimiento, the other was the drug squad,
any time of the day or night there'd be the sound of gunfire.

But I thought he'd come back – I imagined him sheepish, remorseful –
and so I opened up. They sprayed something in my face.

Before I passed out I remember thinking: I hope this isn't acid.
Next thing I knew I woke up twelve hours later, in the night,

lying on the floor. They'd stripped the place.
Not just the hi-fi and jewellery. The furniture, appliances, the lot.

I'd nothing but the clothes I stood there in.
I rang out the neighbour. It seemed she'd watched them carry
    everything out.

There was a Mudanzas truck. Company address and number.
She thought we were moving, or maybe she preferred to think
    we were.

It turned out I still had the car keys and change
in the pocket of my dungarees,

so I got in the car and started driving.
At a light I wound the window down

and a guy pulled a gun and said get out, I need your car.
So I got out, the light turned green, and he drove off.

I sat down in the street and cried, and then I had to laugh (she says)
because it looked as if he'd waited for the light to change.

XI

I took the battered steamer from Stamboul
with a handful of others – a family of Poles,

the father self-effacing, the mother effaced,
their delicate daughter, the daughter's fiancé,

and a sharp young tenebrous Greek with a sketchbook,
like a mortician affecting to be an artist.

The steamer chattered on (says Death) with a ravel of feathering grey
trailing from the smokestack like a scattering of ash

and dolphins, dark as mussel-shells, beside us in the surge,
leaping and thrashing like carp in a friary pond.

I talked to the Greek of matters of local interest –
which fish in the Sea of Marmara made the best eating,

what to beware of when buying Armenian silver,
the reputations of the French and Russians – but after a while

a silence settled between us, and I watched the dolphins again,
busy as sempstresses sewing a bridal gown.

The beautiful daughter was pale. For her sake
the family summered in a southern climate.

At times she would cough, or would seem to catch her breath.
The intended would offer his arm, or a handkerchief,

and horrified disavowal would shine in her eyes,
as if to say it was nothing, she was entirely at one with the world.

On one side Asia rose from the water, on the other Europe.
The dolphins sewed their everlasting shroud.

The steep blue shores with plumes of cypresses
lay in the haze of distance, and the islands shimmered in the sea,

and every so often an eagle sailed over our heads,
crossing from continent to continent.

The way the story has been told (says Death),
the Greek had settled to his drawing, sketchbook on his lap,

the brim of his hat pulled down, his back to the rail,
when one of the ancient mariners, with mischief on his mind,

telling a terrible story as his sort are known to do,
sold the young Polish fellow the thought that the artist was a vampire

and anyone he drew was doomed to die.
Next thing, the sheet had been torn off the pad

and the face of the girl, in wide-eyed funereal charcoal,
stared out as if from a photograph on a grave –

and the men were at each other's throats, and rolling on the deck,
and the girl was yelling, "Not today! I won't have any quarrelling today!"

The way the story's been told, you'd expect her to die.
And so she did, I suppose. In the course of time. Of course she did.

Truth is (says Death), I've no idea what became of them all.
Let's say the youngsters married, and lived happily. Or not.

But some time later I returned. The shorelines of the islands
were strewn with dolphin carcasses. The air was thick to gagging

with the stench of oil in cauldrons as their flesh was rendered down.
And that is how the story always ends.

XII

I threw my Johnson's *Dictionary* out the carriage window –
long time ago (says Death) – and stuck to playing games.

She's trying to make new words
from the letters in *opus posthumous*.

So far she's got *possum* and *opossum*,
pompous, sumptuous, and *stupor*.

She toys with *stupor*,
tongue between her teeth,

and finds the same six letters
spell out *Proust* as well

and *Proust* in turn
consists of *pus* and *rot*.

At which point she sees
she's been using an *r*

that wasn't in the original phrase.
She starts again. *Humus. Sputum. Mush.*

XIII

Lovers re-discover boredom. This is one of those days.
I'm watching *Friends*. And then a shopping channel.

She's been out. To talk to the author of the *Quixote*, it seems.
She asked him to sign her first edition (Nîmes, 1904)

of his monograph on the *characteristica universalis* of Leibniz,
which she told him was far and away the funniest book she'd
    ever read.

– What did he say to that? – What do you think?
Every writer loves to be told he gave pleasure.

He showed her selected treasures from his collection –
d'Annunzio's night-shirt with the notorious hole,

an autograph copy of Colette's *Hamlet on La Cannebière*,
the knickers with which Anatole France had wanted to be buried –

and, as she was leaving, mentioned the sadness
that overwhelmed him when he first beheld *Les Parapluies*.

So many people, and not a single umbrella that wasn't black!
True, she agreed. For it was the case. Unarguably so.

But still she was taken aback to see so many umbrellas crammed
in the stand in his hall. However (she asked him)

could so many of the living have left so many umbrellas behind?
That one (she opened it up) might have been

the very one, the sunnier one, Gene Kelly bought the following day,
having sung and danced his older rainy one away.

That could have served to shelter lovers parting in a parking lot,
pained beyond measure, the raindrops percussive on car-tops
     all around.

And that one, the parasol, ought to be held
in a balancing act on the scalloped basin-edge of a Roman fountain.

It isn't often, the author told her, drooling like a Disney wolf,
that anyone so appreciates my umbrellas.

She furled them, replaced them, abandoned the mystery,
took herself back (so she says) to the present, the clear and
     present world.

XIV

Take Beethoven's quartets, she says – they're stored
in any publisher's warehouse like

potatoes in a cellar. They are things,
like stones in the road, like clods in a field,

like skewers, mouse-pads, pitchers, mobile phones.
– Like fate, free-will, foreknowledge absolute?

– No, those are abstract concepts, the things she means
are, well, *things*. – But what's stored in the warehouse

must be the scores, the paper sheaves with markings,
and not the *music*, not what we think we mean when we say
     "quartets"?

– This is just so much semantics, she says. – But
how is a quartet of Beethoven like a potato or a stone?

The music is abstract, surely? Only the paper
resembles the clods in the field? – Let's start again, she says.

IV

The Truth of Fiction (I)

In the shade on the grass
a writer's telling the story of a man, no longer young or strong,
who carried a magnetic sound recorder,
a prototype developed in Chicago, weighing sixty pounds,
around the crowded DP camps
of Europe under Allied occupation, in the days
when millions were returning to the homes they thought they had,
and millions more were leaving, or were seeking those they'd lost.
The man recorded stories. And the writer
wrote the story of the man. Behind the writer, over there,
a palm has grown out horizontal from the grassy slope,
and, look, along the palm a little girl comes walking on her hands,
a slender golden girl. And now
I'm finding it's becoming hard to know
whether I should watch the girl
or listen to the writer –
both of them require my full attention.
One woman whom the man recorded (so the writer says)
had given her only child, a daughter,
into the care and keeping of a true and trusted friend,
a childless woman, a good woman, to see her through the war. The girl
is turning cart-wheels now,
she's tumbling, rolling down
the bank and shrieking, running up
and rolling down again. And what
became of her? – the daughter? What
became of her? For a year or so (the woman told the man)
it all went well – it seems my daughter flourished – she
was passed off as the daughter of my friend –
but, as her features found their definition,
her face recalled to villagers her Jewish father's face,
and they reported her. You know

the only way that that could end.
I shall not see her in this life again. – Oh no, I want to say,
there must be some mistake – just see,
she's there, the little girl, just see,
there on the palm tree, see, she's dancing
and twirling and stretching up aloft her golden arms in the sun, just see,
and calling to her mother, Look at me!

The Truth of Fiction (II)

She wants to dance to 'Singin' in the Rain'
over and over again, my little daughter –

splashing in puddles, she pauses to explain,
I'm walking on the water!

Author's Note

'The Syrian Bride' began life long ago in an attempt to return to the source tale behind Goethe's poem 'The Bride of Corinth', a story from Phlegon of Tralles set in Syria; the poem changed shape under the pressure of recent events. 'A Carcass' draws upon Baudelaire's poem 'Une Charogne', and on a letter written by Rilke to his wife, Clara Westhoff, on 19 October 1907, in which he claimed that Cézanne could recite the poem word perfect. Sections of 'Foreknowledge Absolute' make various uses of specific texts: II *Alice in Wonderland*; III Hawthorne's 'Wakefield'; IV Clarice Lispector's *crônica* for 16 March 1968; VI Octave Mirbeau's *The Torture Garden*, Kafka's *Metamorphosis* and Dezsö Kostolányi's *Skylark*; VII Jenny Erpenbeck's *The Visitation*; IX Frank O'Hara's 'The Day Lady Died'; XI Jan Neruda's 'The Vampire' and Yashar Kemal's *The Sea-Crossed Fisherman*; XIII Borges's 'Pierre Menard, Author of the *Quixote*' and Undine Gruenter's *Epiphanien, abgeblendet* (number XXVIII); and XIV Heidegger's 'The Origin of the Work of Art'. The writer who appears in 'The Truth of Fiction (I)' is Elliot Perlman, describing the making of *The Street Sweeper* at Adelaide Writers' Week, 2012.

Biographical Note

MICHAEL HULSE grew up in England, the son of an English father from the Potteries and a German mother from near Trier in the Mosel valley. After studying at St. Andrews he lived for twenty-five years in Germany, working in universities, publishing and documentary television, before returning to England in 2002 to teach at the University of Warwick.

His poetry has won him firsts in the National Poetry Competition and the Bridport Poetry Prize (twice), and Eric Gregory and Cholmondeley Awards from the Society of Authors, and has taken him on reading tours of Canada, the US, Mexico, Australia, New Zealand, India, and several European countries.

He has edited the literary quarterlies *Stand, Leviathan Quarterly* and (currently) *The Warwick Review*, co-edited the bestselling anthologies *The New Poetry* and *The Twentieth Century in Poetry*, and in the Nineties was general editor of the Könemann literature classics series and of Arc International Poets.

He has translated more than sixty books from the German, among them works by Goethe, Rilke, Jakob Wassermann, W. G. Sebald, and Nobel Prize winners Elfriede Jelinek and Herta Müller. He is a permanent judge of the Günter Grass Foundation's biennial international literary award, the Albatross Prize, and in 2011 shared a Times Higher Education Award for Excellence and Innovation in the Arts for his work on the Hippocrates poetry and medicine project.

Michael Hulse is married, with one daughter, and lives in Stafford.

Selected titles in Arc Publications'
POETRY FROM THE UK / IRELAND include:

Liz Almond
The Shut Drawer
Yelp!

D M Black
Claiming Kindred

James Byrne
Blood / Sugar

Jonathan Asser
Outside The All Stars

Donald Atkinson
In Waterlight:
Poems New, Selected & Revised

Elizabeth Barrett
A Dart of Green & Blue

Joanna Boulter
Twenty Four Preludes & Fugues on
Dmitri Shostakovich

Thomas A Clark
The Path to the Sea

Tony Curtis
What Darkness Covers
The Well in the Rain
folk

Julia Darling
Sudden Collapses in Public Places
Apology for Absence

Cliff Forshaw
Vandemonian

Linda France
You are Her

Katherine Gallagher
Circus-Apprentice
Carnival Edge

Chrissie Gittins
Armature

Richard Gwyn
Sad Giraffe Café

Glyn Hughes
A Year in the Bull-Box

Michael Haslam
The Music Laid Her Songs in Language
A Sinner Saved by Grace
A Cure for Woodness

Michael Hulse
The Secret History

Brian Johnstone
The Book of Belongings

Joel Lane
Trouble in the Heartland
The Autumn Myth

Herbert Lomas
The Vale of Todmorden
A Casual Knack of Living
(COLLECTED POEMS)

Pete Morgan
August Light

Michael O'Neill
Wheel

Mary O'Donnell
The Ark Builders

Ian Pople
An Occasional Lean-to
Saving Spaces

Paul Stubbs
The Icon Maker

Lorna Thorpe
A Ghost in My House
Sweet Torture of Breathing

Michelene Wandor
Musica Transalpina
Music of the Prophets
Natural Chemistry

Jackie Wills
Fever Tree
Commandments